The Statue of Liberty

by Dana Meachen Rau

Content Adviser: Professor Sherry L. Field, Department of Social Science Education,

College of Education, The University of Georgia

Reading Adviser: Dr. Linda D. Labbo, Department of Reading Education,

College of Education, The University of Georgia

Compass Point Books

Minneapolis, Minnesota

Compass Point Books
3722 West 50th Street, #115
Minneapolis, MN 55410

Visit Compass Point Books on the Internet at *www.compasspointbooks.com* or e-mail your request to
custserv@compasspointbooks.com

Photographs ©: Photo Network, cover; M. Long/Visuals Unlimited, 4; North Wind Picture Archives, 6, 8, 10;
Unicorn Stock Photos/Jeff Greenberg, 12; Photo Network/Esbin-Anderson, 14; Photo Network/Grace Davies, 16;
Lambert/Archive Photos, 18; Hulton Getty/Archive Photos, 20.

Editors: E. Russell Primm and Emily J. Dolbear
Photo Researcher: Svetlana Zhurkina
Photo Selector: Phyllis Rosenberg
Designer: Melissa Voda

Library of Congress Cataloging-in-Publication Data
Rau, Dana Meachen, 1971—
    The Statue of Liberty / by Dana Meachen Rau.
        p. cm. — (Let's see library. Our nation)
    Includes bibliographical references and index.
    Summary: Introduces the history and symbolism of the famous New York City landmark, the Statue of Liberty.
    ISBN 0-7565-0143-1 (hardcover, library binding)
    1. Statue of Liberty (New York, N.Y.)—Juvenile literature. 2. Statue of Liberty (New York, N.Y.)—History—
Juvenile literature. 3. New York (N.Y.)—Buildings, structures, etc.—Juvenile literature. [1. Statue of Liberty (New
York, N.Y.) 2. National monuments. 3. Statues. 4. New York (N.Y.)—Buildings, structures, etc.] I. Title. II. Series.
    F128.64.L6 R38 2002
    974.7'1—dc21   2001002751

Table of Contents

Where Is the Statue of Liberty?

Have you ever visited New York City? The city has many interesting sights. One of the most famous is the Statue of **Liberty**.

The Statue of Liberty is on Liberty Island. This is in New York Harbor. It is a very tall statue of a woman. She is holding a tablet and a torch. Some people call her Lady Liberty. She has stood there for more than 100 years.

◀ *The Statue of Liberty stands in the middle of New York Harbor.*

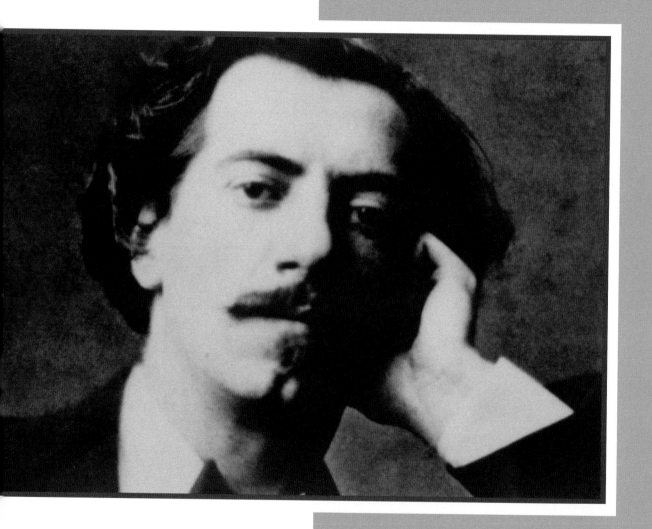

Who Made the Statue of Liberty?

The Statue of Liberty was made by an artist named Frédéric-Auguste Bartholdi. He lived in France.

Bartholdi made statues for places all over France. He loved working on very big statues. He had to cut a special door into the wall of his workshop to get them out.

Why Was the Statue Made?

France had helped the United States fight the Revolutionary War (1775–1783). The leaders and people of the two countries became good friends.

The French people wanted to be sure the Americans would help them if they ever needed help. Bartholdi and other French people thought it would be a good idea to give a gift to the United States.

How Was the Statue Made?

Bartholdi had to make the statue in pieces. First, he made small **models** out of clay. He used math to figure out how big each piece would be.

Lots of workers helped him hammer copper into shapes. The copper was the "skin" of the statue. Then a steel skeleton was built. The workers packed the pieces into crates. They sent the crates to America on a ship.

The Americans built a base for the statue. In 1886, when the crates arrived, workers put the pieces together like a big puzzle.

◄ *Workers make the statue's hand.*

How Big Is the Statue of Liberty?

Look at a picture of the Statue of Liberty. Can you tell how big she is? If the Statue of Liberty stood next to a building, her crown would reach the twenty-second floor!

Now hold up your finger. How long is it? The Statue of Liberty's finger is about as tall as the ceiling in your house. Her nose is taller than you are. Her eyes are as wide as your desk. She weighs about the same as forty elephants.

Do you know anyone bigger than Lady Liberty?

◄ *The Statue of Liberty's nose is taller than you are!*

What Do the Parts of the Statue of Liberty Mean?

Many parts of the statue have a special meaning. For example, Lady Liberty is stepping forward with her left foot. A broken chain lies at her feet. This shows that she is free.

Her crown has seven spikes. These spikes stand for the seven seas and seven **continents** of Earth. Her right hand holds up a torch. This shows she is sending her message to the whole world.

◀ *The Statue of Liberty's right hand holds up a torch.*

How Can You See the Statue of Liberty?

You can visit the Statue of Liberty. First, you take a ferry to Liberty Island. There is a museum in the base of the statue.

You can climb 192 steps to the top of the base of the statue. Are you tired yet? Next you can climb 162 more steps to the crown. That is a total of 354 steps! You can look out to see the city and the harbor below.

◀ *Visitors take a ferry to get to the statue.*

Did the Statue of Liberty Ever Need to Be Fixed?

Over time, the statue turned green from the salty air and windy weather. It was covered with holes and rust. President Ronald Reagan put together a team of people to fix the statue.

The statue was fixed in time for its 100th birthday. People celebrated on July 4, 1986, with fireworks and music.

◄ *Workers repaired the statue in 1986.*

What Does the Statue of Liberty Mean to People?

The Statue of Liberty was very important to **immigrants**. Immigrants are people who come from other countries to live in America. Many of them saw the statue from ships as they arrived.

Many people think of America and the importance of **freedom** when they see the Statue of Liberty. What do you think of?

◄ *The Statue of Liberty gives hope to all people who want to be free.*

Glossary

continents—the seven largest land areas on Earth

freedom—the right to do and say what you wish

immigrants—people who leave one country to settle in another

liberty—freedom

model—a small copy of something

tablet—a piece of stone with words carved on it

torch—a light that helps people see in the dark

Did You Know?

• Frédéric-Auguste Bartholdi was born in 1834 and died in 1904.

• Alexandre Gustave Eiffel built the Statue of Liberty's skeleton. He also built a famous monument in Paris called the Eiffel Tower.

• Bartholdi designed the face of the Statue of Liberty after his mother.

Want to Know More?

At the Library

Bunting, Eve. *A Picnic in October*. San Diego: Harcourt Brace and Company, 1999.

Curlee, Lynn. *Liberty*. New York: Atheneum Books for Young Readers, 2000.

Marx, David F. *New York City*. Danbury, Conn.: Children's Press, 1999.

On the Web

The Statue of Liberty
http://www.endex.com/gf/buildings/liberty/liberty.html
For general facts and information, a picture gallery, and recent news about the Statue of Liberty

National Park Service Statue of Liberty National Monument
http://www.nps.gov/stli/
For a complete history of the park and information about visiting the monument

The Statue of Liberty Photo Tour
http://www.nyctourist.com/liberty1.htm
For a photo tour to the monument, through the museum, and to the top of the statue

Through the Mail

Statue of Liberty National Monument
Liberty Island
New York, NY 10004
For information about the Statue of Liberty National Monument including how to visit

On the Road

The Statue of Liberty National Monument and the
Ellis Island Immigration Museum
Ferries leave from Battery Park in New York City and from Liberty State Park in Jersey City, New Jersey.

Index

About the Author
Dana Meachen Rau is the author of more than fifty books for children, including historical fiction, storybooks, nonfiction, biographies, and early readers. Dana also works as a children's book editor and illustrator and lives with her husband, Chris, and son, Charlie, in Farmington, Connecticut.